WHY & WHAT

A BRIEF INTRODUCTION

TO

CHRISTIANITY

DOUGLAS JONES

canonpress
Moscow, Idaho

For the brothers,
Russell, Curtiss, Joseph, and John
and for Dana Collins

Published by Canon Press
P.O. Box 8729, Moscow, ID 83843
800.488.2034 | www.canonpress.com

Douglas M. Jones III, *Why and What:*
A Brief Introduction to Christianity
Copyright © 1997, 2010 Douglas M. Jones III
Second Edition.

Cover design by Rachel Hoffmann and Laura Storm.
Interior design by Laura Storm.
Printed in the United States of America.

Library of Congress Cataloging-in-Publication Data
Jones, Douglas, 1963-
    Why and what : a brief introduction to Christianity / Douglas Jones. -- 2nd ed.
    p. cm.
    ISBN-13: 978-1-59128-023-1 (booklet)
    ISBN-10: 1-59128-023-0 (booklet)
    1. Christianity. I. Title.
    BR121.3.J66 2007
    230--dc22

                                        2007018011

10 11 12 13 14 15 16 17   9 8 7 6 5 4 3

contents

radical mistakes

CHAPTER 1

Imagine that you are mistaken about everything you hold dear. Suppose you wake up one morning and clearly realize that your long-held, day-to-day views of nature, social values, and self are obviously mistaken. Common things that you have seen for years take on a whole new light. The world hasn't changed, but different things stand out in odd ways. Things you once adored are now utterly disgusting. Things you once hated now command your deepest loyalty. You can now see through your motives and rationalizations in a way hidden before. How could you have been so naive?

Could one really be so radically deceived about the world after all these years? We may not often think about it, but most people do in fact assume that millions of others are out to lunch in just this way. For example, probably much of the world believes, rightly or wrongly, that millions of zealous Muslims are seriously disconnected from reality. And millions of third-world animists, slavishly trying to balance numerous life forces in trees and rocks and heads, fare no better on reality checks. Even postmodernist types who pretend to deny any single reality or truth are usually the first to insist that the vast millions of us who believe in reality and truth are terribly mistaken about *the* world.

Some can easily write off "fanatics," but why can't a more mundane, common-sensical, middle-of-the-road view be equally deceived about the world? After all, most people with "sane," moderate views acquired those views in the same way that most "fanatics" acquired theirs—living in a community where those views seem obvious. Fanatics don't usually look like fanatics within their own communities. There, they appear rather mundane and average. To them, *you* are the fanatic, wildly at odds with reality.

Most people hold the beliefs they do because they picked them up along the way from people they trusted— parents, friends, media, maybe even from some zealous college instructor. But over millennia, many parents and zealous college instructors have proven themselves terribly mistaken. Real deception never looks strange when you're on the inside.

The kind of deception I'm suggesting isn't the rather unbelievable sort, like being mistaken about whether your left thumb is really an African elephant. The more interesting and plausible kind of radical deception involves less obvious, even invisible things, like moral standards and rules of reasoning and assumptions about how the world works. If people are wrong about these sorts of things, then they could be radically mistaken but go along with the flow of life in the short term without running into any corners. They might only recognize their horrible mistake in the long run, when it all starts to fall apart. But then it could be dangerously late.

Now add to all this the fact that anyone's years on earth has really been very few. And the time any of us spends thinking about the world is relatively minute compared to all that there is to understand. Given all this, then, isn't it even *likely* that most people, maybe even you, are indeed radically deceived about the world? Considering how many and how easily people are deceived, it doesn't seem that wild a conjecture.

In fact, people's actions often reveal more about their likely deception than their words. For example, whenever you do something like go to a grocery store to buy milk, you reveal many things about yourself. When you first walk up to the grocery store, you assume that you and the store are two different things, not one, thus showing your rejection of most Eastern and New Age religions. When you walk down that same dairy aisle and select the same kind of milk, you assume that the world is not chaotic, but orderly, regular, and divided into set kinds of things. When you stand in line with others, expecting others to respect your space and person, you reveal your rejection of moral relativism and your deep trust in absolute ethical norms. When you calculate your available change, compare the price of the milk, and make the exchange with the clerk at the register, you engage in a complex array of thought processes involving nonmaterial rules of reasoning, thus showing your rejection of materialism and evolution.

In short, when you do something as mundane as buying milk, you accept and reject all sorts of views. You act like you reject many popular religions and scientific claims. In fact, given the sum of what you assume and reject just when buying milk, you act like you believe that you live in the world described by Christianity. The world depicted above suggests complexities and contours of reality that are only supplied in Christianity. If Christianity weren't true, then such things as simple as milk buying would appear to be impossible. Now, you may openly reject Christianity, but you certainly act like it is true and that your non-Christianity is false. Why such self-deception? Why don't you just confess what you appear to assume?

Non-Christian thought has no cogent answer for such evident and world-encompassing self-deception, but Christianity does. The Christian Scriptures explain that the world is in an abnormal state, due to the destructiveness of our sin. We have rebelled against a holy and gracious God, and so we try to make up grand scenarios in order to evade Him. Such evasion isn't a marginal error. It is concerted warfare against our Creator, and it deserves divine capital punishment. The alternative to such self-deceptive evasion is to embrace the mercy found in Christ, the God-given substitute sent to take our punishment so that we can be reconciled and at peace with God. That's the heart of Christianity— peace with God through Christ's work, with no more radical self-deception about the world.

Could you be radically mistaken in your non-Christian outlook? It looks likely. You profess non-Christianity, but assume Christianity. Think about Christ's work the next time you go to buy some milk.

non-Christian hypocrisy

CHAPTER 2

Consider the discussion of radical self-deception from another angle. Countless non-Christians have claimed to reject the Christian faith by gaping at the scandalous lives of many professing Christians. But isn't the radical self-deception embraced by non-Christians also a form of hypocrisy?

When professing Christians display their hypocrisy, we bristle that they so widely broadcast their alleged commitment to Christ but act as if He were an empty fiction. Their open adulteries or gossip or lack of reverence show that they don't really believe that God is their near and present judge. No criminal defendant in a human court would make nasty faces at his judge or dance a rude jig around the courtroom while the judge prepares a sentence. A Christian hypocrite is one who professes that the judge's bench is filled but acts like it's really vacant.

But non-Christians can be even more hypocritical. They claim to be very confident that there is no judge, courtroom, or any law, but they spend their whole lives revealing that they know that the judge is really sitting there watching. Even the most blasphemous opponents of the "alleged" judge still demand to have injustices retributed, still demand that we reason according to the set rules of the court, and still demand that they are innocent of any crimes. They verbally deny the existence of the judge but show that they really do know that the bench is filled. They don't have the courage of their convictions, because, perhaps, they know those convictions are false.

For example, non-Christians committed to the mythology of evolution, an impersonal cosmos grinding out valueless, buzzing matter, still chirpily insist on human rights, the value of all living things, and universal rules of reason and toleration. Pure hypocrisy! Non-Christians committed to a New Age or Eastern oneness of all things still insist on looking both ways before they cross a street. More hypocrisy. Their actions belie their professions.

In Romans 1:18 and following, the Apostle Paul famously describes non-Christians as those who know the truth of the Christian Creator and Judge but "suppress the truth in unrighteousness." God has made the knowledge of Himself so clear "that they are without excuse" (Rom. 1:20). They know it, and they show it, among other ways, in their hypocrisy. They act like they live in a Christian universe, even though they deny it. Because of this ingratitude, this suppression of the truth, Paul tells us that "the wrath of God is revealed from heaven" against them, for "although they knew God, they did not glorify Him as God, nor were they thankful, but became futile in their thoughts" (Rom. 1:18, 21).

When he was in Athens before the esteemed intellectuals of his day, Paul pointed out how desperately religious they were. Their idolatries revealed a deep, culpable knowledge of God, though they tried to deny it by exchanging the truth of God for a lie (Rom. 1:25). Paul criticized their philosophies at every step of the way, showing their inadequacies and folly. We can ask a similar question. If a non-Christian view of things is true, then there is no reason for respecting others, loving our children, opposing injustices, feeling guilty, preferring truth, reasoning, or staying alive. Non-Christians do all these things, and all these things and more testify to their knowledge of the true God. Hypocrisy seems to overwhelm them. Their own lives so clearly reveal that they know their views are false and that Christianity is true.

faith is rationality

CHAPTER 3

The previous arguments (from two angles) suggest that even the most skeptical non-Christians act like closet Christians. The fact that we all assume the truth of a Christian view of reality is one good and broad *reason* among many for embracing Christ. But from many sides we are told that reason and faith conflict, that they are two opposed means of acquiring knowledge. Reason, in this broad sense, is the set of rules of thought that we ought to use to evaluate and extend our beliefs, exiling absurdities, contradictions, and unsupported claims. Faith, in contrast, is the rejection of these highest norms of thought in order to blindly embrace the dictates of authority and revel in absurdities. Or so the story goes.

Consequently, non-Christians often accuse Christians of irrationality for giving any place to faith, and many Christians often reject any place for reason and making irrationality ("faith" as they see it) the hallmark of the Christian religion. But it seems that all these views are misguided, and their common error is that they mischaracterize *rationality*.

What is rationality? Many theories are available. For example, some contend that rationality is choosing the best means for a desired end. But this understanding quickly becomes unmanageable—we could make every action rational by making it a desired end in itself. I think another understanding of rationality is more helpful. We might find broader agreement by understanding rationality, in a basic sense, *as conforming one's beliefs and actions to the highest rules of truth.* The "conforming" aspect retains the ability to exclude absurdities, those things that violate the highest rules of truth. The "highest" aspect directs us ultimately to those rules that serve as the final court of appeal, those that have a veto over all other rules. The "truth" aspect points us to the nature of the world, to reality and not just our own imaginations. Reality determines rationality. A rational person, then, is one who lives in accordance with the supreme rules of truth.

When some non-Christian claims to follow "reason" and reject "faith," he aims to obey the rules of truth that govern reality, maybe something like the laws of logic or scientific methods or something like that. He may imagine that he is doing something completely different than the person devoted to the Christian God, but in truth, the two are following the same procedure. They both seek to obey the highest rules of truth. Christian faith doesn't ask us to act blindly, seeking to go contrary to reality. It seeks to follow the same procedure as the person devoted to rationality, though of course the two appeal to opposing ultimate standards.

To see this better, consider the case of Abraham, that ancient father of Judaism and Christianity.† In the traditional dispute over reason and faith, Abraham would surely be classified as a model of faith. The Bible tells us that God called Abraham as His own and promised him descendants and a land, though Abraham was then childless, and the land was occupied by powerful and hostile peoples. But contrary to all the prevailing evidence that descendants are unlikely if you yourself lack a child, and contrary to all the evidence against a solitary, elderly gentleman beating back a host of hostile armies, Abraham *believed in the Lord* (Gen. 15:6). Years later, when the Lord finally declared his wife's upcoming pregnancy, though she was nearing one hundred years of age, Abraham believed, trusting God's promise, contrary to the expert opinions about persons who are past childbearing years being able to bear children. Even later in Abraham's life, after the birth of this long-promised son, God directed Abraham to go on an excursion to sacrifice that same son, Isaac. But instead of being "rational" as some take it, explaining to God that corpses don't make good fathers of many descendants, Abraham had faith, believing the absurdity that God was able to raise his son from the dead in order to fulfill His promise of many descendants.

In all this, Abraham showed himself to be a model of faith. But from a non-Christian perspective, Abraham, each step of the way, was exceedingly irrational and probably dangerous to society. (Social workers would surely have been put out by his little excursion

† I am indebted here to John Frame's comments on Abraham and the nature of reason.

with Isaac.) Abraham's conclusions would certainly be at odds with those recommended by our established scientific community. From this non-Christian view, Abraham, as a model of faith, is also a model of irrationality.

But given the understanding of rationality discussed above—conforming our thoughts and actions to the highest rules of truth—Abraham was not irrational in the slightest. If Abraham's worldview is correct, then Abraham's God reigns as the standard of truth high above any helpful insights from philosophers and scientists. In biblical reality, there are no norms of thought over and above those of the supreme person of God. Moreover, if that view is correct, then Abraham is not only a model of faith but also a model of rationality, a devoted "rationalist," conforming his life to the highest rules of truth. Abraham would have been foolish and supremely *irrational* to believe contrary to God's promise.

So, in the end, the supposed hostility between reason and faith dissolves in an interesting way. Faith and reason are not enemies but identical. They both seek conformity to the highest rule of truth. And, as we've already seen above, though non-Christians profess to obey their own alleged rules of truth, not one of them does so faithfully. They all act as though the Christian view of reality is true, all the while denying it. That is true irrationality. That is true blind faith. In stark contrast, Christianity rejects blind faith and calls us to bow before the Christian God, the God of Abraham, Isaac, and Joseph—the supreme standard of thought and life, to whom all rational people ought to conform.

the Jewishness
of Christianity

CHAPTER 4

Having seen a small part of the "why" of Christianity, let's turn to the "what," the contents of Christianity. One of the best ways of beginning to think about
the nature of Christianity is to think of it in the light
of Judaism. Today, we so often think of Judaism and
Christianity as two distinct religions, almost like Bud-
dhism and Islam. But early Christianity never saw itself in that way. The earliest Christians saw themselves
as faithful Jews simply following Jewish teachings. In
fact, the first main dispute in the Christian church was
whether non-Jews, the Gentiles, could even be a part
of Christianity!

Christianity self-consciously saw itself as the continuing outgrowth, the fulfillment, of true Judaism. As such,
Christianity didn't start in first century but long before
with King David, Moses, Abraham, and ultimately the
first man, Adam. Everything in older Judaism was build-
ing up and pointing to the work of Jesus Christ. Over
and over, the early disciples explained that Christ was
the fulfillment of the ancient promises of Judaism.

When Mary, Jesus' mother, learned that she was to give birth to the promised Messiah, she didn't think that this would be some new, unconnected event, beginning only in the first century. No, she sang of God's ancient promises to Abraham and Israel: "He has helped His servant Israel, in remembrance of His mercy, as he spoke to our fathers, to Abraham and to his seed forever" (Lk. 1:54–55; cf. Lk. 1:68–74). And Christ's Apostles declared the message that "Christ has redeemed us from the curse of the law, having become a curse for us . . . that the blessing of Abraham might come upon the Gentiles in Christ Jesus. . . . And if you are Christ's, then you are Abraham's seed, and heirs according to the promise" (Gal. 3:13–14, 29; cf. Acts 3:20–26). Christianity is ancient Judaism fulfilled, and, as such, Christianity is the world's oldest faith, dating back to the very beginning of creation.

So when we start thinking about Christianity, we have to understand its very Jewish roots. We should assume that Christianity ought to look and sound like Judaism except when it explicitly claims to change something. We should expect that the Scriptures, institutions, basic principles, laws, meditations, family life, etc. of Judaism would carry over into Christianity, unless Christ, the final prophet, authoritatively changed a practice. For example, since Christ is the reality to which all the ancient Judaic animal sacrifices were but a picture, a foreshadow, when Christ comes as the truly effective sacrifice, we no longer need the ineffective pictures. Thus, animal sacrifices have now ceased, having been fulfilled by their goal, Christ Himself.

Christianity's Jewishness is pervasive indeed. Probably one of the most central notions of Christianity now often closely associated with Judaism is the notion of a *covenant*. We don't often hear talk of covenants in our day, but we really can't understand the heights and depths and riches of Christianity if we don't have a good grasp of a covenant. To start, a covenant is a special kind of relationship between persons. People can be related by friendship, employment contracts, geographical location, citizenship, etc., but a covenant *ties people together in a bond of mutual promise that involves conditions of blessing and cursing.*

A covenant is so important in grasping basic Christianity because the Bible makes clear that this is the sort of relationship that God chose to have with humans. He may have chosen another kind of relationship, like a labor contract, but He didn't. He chose to bind Himself to us by a covenant. A covenant is intended to be a very intimate, merciful, and gracious kind of relationship. It is intended to be a unique bond of friendship, a protection for the weak, a comfort for the lost. A covenant is supposed to be like the very best marriage and like the warmest father-child bond.

This special covenantal bond that God instituted between humans and Himself is the core around which the history of the world develops. We'll see more of the details about this covenantal relationship in a moment, but the broad picture of the Christian message is that God's covenantal relationship with humans proceeds through three distinct episodes over all of history: *creation, Fall,* and *redemption.* All of the Christian faith can be handily summarized by these three periods.

We might also think of these pivotal periods in terms of the best relationship *gained, lost,* and *regained* or paradise gained, paradise lost, and paradise regained, if we understand "paradise" primarily in terms of a peaceful, harmonious relationship between God and humans. Humanity was once at peace with God, then it rebelled; God is now mercifully reconciling the world to Himself through Christ. One contemporary Christian scholar summarized this Christian message very well when he said:

> The essential teaching of the Christian faith is that reconciliation has been effected between God and sinful man through Jesus Christ, and that this new relation between God and man is a present possibility for those outside the church, and a present actuality for those in its bounds.[†]

This summary is well worth meditating on as we try to get a handle on Christianity. Creation/Fall/redemption is also a way to summarize the message of the entire Bible, the supreme norm for all Christian thought and practice. The first book of the Bible, Genesis, reveals much about creation and the Fall, and the rest of the Bible, Old and New Covenants or Testaments, is taken up with the glorious work of regaining paradise, of reconciliation between God and man, most conclusively through the work of Christ. So when you try to get a handle on the immensity of the Christian Bible or Scripture, start by seeing it outlined in terms of creation, Fall, and redemption.

[†] Alister McGrath, *Iustitia Dei,* Vol. I (Cambridge: Cambridge University Press, 1993), 1.

Though you might be familiar with the Christian notions of creation, Fall, and redemption, you might be surprised to discover some misconceptions along the way. Consider the following overview of each of these aspects of Christianity.

paradise given:
God and creation

CHAPTER 5

According to popular, twentieth-century dogma, no thinking person is supposed to reject the theory of evolution, the view that living things developed gradually as a result of the interaction of chance and selection. But the mythology behind evolutionary theory is very old, and biblical faith has always battled this religion. For thousands of years, this quaint tale of evolution has regularly brightened the eyes of small tribal children everywhere, but only in the last century did those holding intellectual power insist that we all actually believe this evolution myth as literal truth. These evolutionary fundamentalists, those who maintain that this ancient emanation-from-earth myth should be taken literally, knew they were pushing more of an ideological agenda than pursuing simple science. They had a great philosophical drive to jettison creationism, regardless of the evidence.

The same irrationalism prevails in much of the scientific community today. One recent non-Christian critic of evolutionary theory noted "as the biological community considers Darwinian theory to be established beyond doubt. . . . then dissent becomes by definition ir-rational and hence especially irritating if the dissenters claim to be presenting a rational critique. . . . [N]owa-days it is heretical to question the idea of evolution."[†] Nonetheless, he and others have and will continue to raise considerable doubts about evolutionary theory, contending that Darwin's general theory is still

> a highly speculative hypothesis entirely without direct factual support and very far from that self-evident axiom some of its more aggressive advo-cates would have us believe. . . . Ultimately the Darwinian theory of evolution is no more nor less than the great cosmogenic myth of the twentieth century. . . . [I]t satisfies the same deep psycho-logical need for an all-embracing explanation of the origin of the world which has motivated all the cosmogenic myth makers of the past.[‡]

With so much ideological pressure to believe such an ancient myth, we might expect a little more skepticism from the broader scientific community, but the desire for an evolutionary escape runs deep.

Faithful Christianity has never been tempted to ac-commodate this alien religion since evolutionary theory is not limited to just the question of origins; its impli-cations seek to undermine every aspect of a Christian view of reality—creation, Fall, and redemption.

In its biblical context, the truth of creation—God's creation of the world and its inhabitants, out of nothing,

---

[†] Michael Denton, *Evolution: A Theory in Crisis* (Bethesda: Adler & Adler, 1986), 76.

[‡] Ibid., 358.

by the power of His command alone—reveals much to us about the nature of the Christian God. Consider the following:

Creation reveals a fundamental distinction between God and man: In so many religions, humans and the world are outgrowths of a divine being. For them, God and man are on par; they are made of the same stuff and bow to the same rules. This fits in nicely with the human imagination's desire to make a god after its own likeness. But in the Bible's teaching on creation, God and man are very different in fundamental ways. We're not made of the same kind of stuff, and we shouldn't expect God's ways to imitate ours. We shouldn't expect Him to be fully comprehensible or accountable to our limited ways of thinking. He is the Creator, and we are the created: "'For My thoughts are not your thoughts, nor are your ways My ways,' says the LORD. 'For as the heavens are higher than the earth, so are My ways higher than your ways, and My thoughts than your thoughts'" (Is. 55:8–9).

Creation reveals God's sovereignty over all things: Scripture shows that God made *all* things, not just many or most. Therefore everything in creation stands under His power. Nothing, no fate or forces or personal powers stand above His power. He made them all, "in heaven and . . . on earth, visible and invisible, whether thrones or dominions or principalities or powers. All things were created through Him and for Him" (Col. 1:16). As Creator and ruler, everything is under His control, and no one can thwart His plans: "No one can restrain His hand or say to Him, 'What have You done?'" (Dan. 4:35).

Creation reveals God's right to be glorified in all things: God created all things for His purposes, His glory, not ours. This sounds arrogant in a culture like ours in which we exert every effort to gain our own glory and prestige. It *is* arrogant for a human to demand glory but not for the sovereign Creator of all things. Since He didn't make life for our purposes but for His, everything should be directed to glorify Him: "You are worthy, O Lord, to receive glory and honor and power; for you created all things, and by Your will they exist and were created" (Rev. 4:11). Christianity calls us to look away from ourselves and give glory where it is truly due: "Whether you eat or drink, or whatever you do, do all to the glory of God" (1 Cor. 10:31).

Creation reveals God's lordship and our servant-hood: We regularly acknowledge that the creator of an object owns and controls the thing created. Scripture speaks of God as the master potter and His creation as the clay formed by Him: "Will the thing formed say to him who formed it, 'Why have you made me like this?' Does not the potter have power over the clay?" (Rom. 9:20–21). As creatures, God owns us and has the *right* to direct us in His paths, and we have the obligation to obey His commands: "You shall love the Lord your God with all your heart, with all your soul, and with all your strength" (Deut. 6:4). As a true lord, sovereign above all rule, His authority is beyond question. He is the *final court of appeal* on all things, since He rules "far above all principality and power and might and dominion, and every name that is named, not only in this age but also in that which is to come" (Eph. 1:21).

Creation reveals God's goodness: God doesn't need man or owe man anything. Yet He created us and gave us a beautiful creation to tend and tame. He gave us ocean sunsets, golden plains, snowy crests, and star-jeweled nights. He gave us air and water, tasty foods and soothing drinks, loved ones and creativity, and so much more—even to those who hate Him. And even more, He declared that this creation of His, this *material* world, was good (Gen. 1:31), not something to avoid and hold in low esteem, but a material world to rejoice in with thanksgiving (1 Tim. 4:3–4). Creation and God's continuing support of it speak loudly of God's goodness to everyone, His friends and enemies alike, and our debt to Him: "When I consider Your heavens, the work of Your fingers, The moon and the stars, which You have ordained. What is man that you are mindful of him? . . . And you have crowned Him with glory and honor" (Ps. 8:3–5).

Creation reveals God's covenantal relationship to all mankind: In creating all things, God also created especially unique beings, humans. He created us as those creatures who bear His image, unlike all the others. Humans reflect some of God's characteristics, and, therefore, are set apart for a special protection and closeness with God Himself. He created us to be different from each other, male and female, for His purposes. He commanded us to work and rest and marry and produce children (Gen. 1, 2). But best of all, in our initial state, we were in close harmony with the sovereign God. The God Who was so far above everything was also so very close to us; He dwelt with us.

Most importantly for everything else that follows in history, God related to the first man, Adam, in a special way, a covenantal way. As we saw above, every covenant is a relationship between persons in which both sides have promises to keep, like a marriage. Unlike a covenant between two equals, the covenants God made with humans are covenants between *unequals*, like that between a master and a servant or a conquering king and his new people. In this kind of covenant, the lord, on His own, sets all the terms for the covenant. He determines the promises, conditions, commandments, blessings, curses, etc. for Himself and His servants.

God's covenant with Adam has all the parts of a covenant that later go by that name explicitly, but the truly beautiful part of this covenant between God and man is that God doesn't impose the covenant like a warlord or a slave driver. He institutes it like the best father, one seeking the best interests and protection of his offspring. A newborn child doesn't set any terms or conditions on his relationship with his parents. It's all up to the parents to tend, nurture, and discipline. In the same way, the sovereign Creator embraced Adam, giving him all the blessings of the earth, family life, and work, and He promised him the blessing of peace and harmony with Himself, if Adam would remain faithful to his gracious maker. If Adam rejected God's goodness, going against Adam's own interests, then all peace and harmony would be lost, and alienation would prevail.

Now what makes this covenantal relationship so central to everything else in history is that Adam wasn't just acting for himself. Central to covenantal thinking is the notion of *representation,* the position of standing as the accountable substitute for others. We're probably most familiar with this in terms of politics. In the American system, we vote for representatives whom we send away to be our legal voice. They vote in our place, as legal representatives of our group. When they act, we are acting in them. Similarly, we can again think of covenantal representation in a marriage or a parental bond. In a biblical family, the father and husband is the covenant head of his home. He stands as the representative agent for the best interests of the family. His judgment, whether good or ill, is the representative judgment of the family. When he acts, they act in him. In our day of cultural breakdown, individualism and democracy in the family have tried to eclipse this notion of representation; nonetheless, the reality stands, and its consequences remain.

In a similar way, Adam, the family head, the legal representative of the whole human race acted in our place. His faithfulness as our representative could pass on the eternal blessing of harmony and peace with God. Tragically, though, instead of faithful gratitude for God's goodness, Adam, our representative, *rebelled*.

paradise lost:
human rebellion

CHAPTER 6

One of the best ways to make people abandon an idea is to get even more people to ridicule it. The Fall of man has long been the butt of movie and television jokes, and the conspiracy to trivialize it has succeeded for the gullible. But instead of caricaturing Adam and Eve as naked simpletons munching fruit, we should see their faces in the culture of death engulfing us. Whatever you find most appalling—government tanks crushing children or the weeping of a battered wife—in *that* you should see the face of Adam's rebellion. Violence and hatred against the innocent is never funny, not even in the movies. The ugliness of losing paradise is that in Adam we are the aggressors against a good and holy God.

The Fall and Original Sin

Amidst all the overwhelming blessings of the garden, God also gave Adam a simple command of faithfulness, as was God's right, and Adam chose futility for the human race. The enemy in the form of a serpent appealed to envy, an appeal so common in our own day, to turn Adam and Eve from God. The enemy undermined God's word by suggesting that Adam and Eve were competent judges, in themselves, over the word of the sovereign Creator, the final court of all appeal. Once they bought that assumption, their rebellion was complete. Adam attempted to abdicate his headship and personal responsibility by blaming his wife and God, anyone but himself, another evasion that currently pervades our own culture so destructively.

The double-edged truth about covenants and representatives is that they may bring us blessings *or curses*. Immoral votes by our legislative representatives are *our* votes. Their poor judgments reflect ours, and, therefore, we rightly bear the consequences for our representative's failings, even if we didn't vote for that representative. Similarly, the children often bear the sins of the father. If the father destroys a family name by His immoral activity, the children bear that shame too. They not only bear the father's shame, they regularly continue to imitate the father's unrighteousness throughout their lives. In a stronger covenantal sense, Adam's rebellion was *our* rebellion. His guilt was imputed or attributed to us because of his representative status. When Adam rejected God, the whole human race rejected God and embraced spiritual death: "in Adam all die" (1 Cor. 15:22). And we continue to bear that guilty shame from the day we are born. We are born alienated from God by Adam's guilt imputed to us, and because of this we are born with God's justified wrath against us.

Not only are we born guilty before God, we are also born with a natural tendency toward sin, a tendency that afflicts every aspect of our being—emotions, intellect, will, etc. This pollution is all encompassing like death. We're told that the unbelieving mind "is death" (Rom. 8:6), "being dead in [its] trespasses" (Col. 2:13). Physical death distorts every aspect of our being, and spiritual death does the same. Similarly, Scripture describes this pollution of sin as slavery, that state of having one's entire being under the rule of another: "everyone who commits sin is a slave of sin" (Jn. 8:34), "serving various lusts and pleasures, living in malice and envy" (Tit. 3:3). Besides death and slavery, the Bible also describes life apart from God as blindness: "their understanding [is] darkened, alienated from the life of God" (Eph. 4:18), so that "men loved darkness rather than the light" (Jn. 3:19). Blind, enslaved, and dead rebels are in no place to pull themselves up by their bootstraps to try to please God. Only God can heal spiritual blindness, shatter the bonds of slavery, and raise the dead. Only He can turn His enemies into His friends.

The Fall and Actual Sin

But humans haven't just rested in bearing Adam's covenantal guilt and the ingrained pollution of sin. We have excelled in working out our own actual rebellion against God by our lies, adulteries, hatreds, vanities, blasphemies, idolatries, and envies. Adam may have started the rebellion, but his offspring made sure it continued in full force.

How do we know what sin is? The Scripture explains that "sin is lawlessness" (1 Jn. 3:4). That is, God

has revealed to mankind His standards of holy character, and any violation or failure to meet those standards
of holiness is sin, rebellion against God. So, violations
of the Ten Commandments, in overt action or hidden
motives, are sin, as is the failure to love one another
from the heart and to glorify God in all things.

Part of our rebellion is to minimize sin so that only
those outrageous sins—like murder and theft—count
as "really bad" sins. This is convenient but false. We
needn't be serial killers or thieves to rebel against God.
We rebel every day, in every thought, word, and deed
that denies His glory and seeks to trust in our own
work. God's standards of righteousness are so high that
no one escapes, not the sweet-hearted elderly person
down the street or the popular moral crusader against
injustices. God's standards are far more concerned with
the deeper motives of the heart, where our sin really lies,
rather than mere external actions done for everyone
to see. The murderer openly displays his rebellion, but
that kind, sweet person merely suppresses his or her
rebellion deep inside. Neither fool God. Both will give
an account, and without God's solution, both will face
God's righteous wrath.

In our state of rebellion, we have no hope in our own
strength. We are dead in our sin, impotent to restore
our relationship with God and impotent to turn away
His just wrath. Our natural inclination is to oppose
God, and because of that, no one is open-minded or
neutral about God. The basic desire of the sinful heart
is to dethrone God and enthrone ourselves, however
subtly we try to whitewash our motives. Even our best
efforts at good works—giving to charities, fighting

injustices, caring for a relative—are horribly unacceptable substitutes for the holiness God requires. God doesn't grade on a curve. He accepts only perfect righteousness, which only He can supply.

The Fall and the Divine Antithesis

Adam's rebellion didn't just enslave individuals to sin. It brought rebellion to entire cultures. Immediately after the Fall, God Himself imposed a permanent hostility between two cultures, the culture of God's enemies and the culture of God's friends, when He declared to the enemy: "I will put enmity [hostility] between you and the woman, and between your seed and her seed" (Gen. 3:15). The seed of the serpent—his rebellious heirs throughout history—and the seed of the woman—her faithful heirs throughout history—would be in spiritual combat until the close of history.

This sharp division or antithesis starts at the Fall and develops through the Old and New Covenants of Scripture. Adam's immediate offspring split into two opposing factions and fathered cultures that continue to battle through Noah's time, Abraham's time, Israel's time, Christ's time, and through to our own day and beyond. It's a relentless spiritual division with no peaceful coexistence possible. As the Apostle Paul declared: "For what fellowship has righteousness with lawlessness? And what communion has light with darkness? . . . Or what part has a believer with an unbeliever? And what agreement has the temple of God with idols?" (2 Cor. 6:14–16).

From the very beginning, God commanded His people to remain faithful and separate from the seed of the serpent. They must refuse to imitate and compromise with an enemy at total war with God. Compromising or abandoning a biblical outlook for another is like deserting a victorious army to join the ranks of disarmed rebels. For their own hope, God directs the faithful to distinguish their thinking and acting from those outlooks that oppose God's work. They are to seek to understand the world and all its workings through the description of the sovereign God, who knows it best.

But, of course, neither Israel of old nor its development into the Christian church has always remained uncompromised. At various times in history, those professing to be faithful have chosen to fight with enemy weapons and philosophies. They have tried to make biblical faith tasty to the enemy by futilely trying to mix the antithetical outlooks of the seed of the woman and the serpent. Sadly, this attempt at compromise is what has infected Roman Catholicism and Eastern Orthodoxy for centuries. They have abandoned their scriptural, Jewish roots in favor of largely pagan Greek philosophies covered over with Christian terminology. Much of contemporary Protestantism has compromised in similar ways, but classical Protestantism over the centuries has been the concerted effort, with ups and downs, to embrace the biblical faith of Abraham, Moses, David, and its fulfillment in Christ and His Apostles.

This spiritual antithesis between Christianity and its opponents continues on many contemporary fronts as well. The divine antithesis imposed by God at the Fall requires some very stark divisions at times, primarily between those seeking to be faithful to Christ and those opposing Him. Some opponents fight Christianity by trying to do away with any divisions among humans—true/false, good/evil, male/female, rich/poor, guilty/innocent, human/nonhuman, Creator/creature, etc. This ancient ploy, begun at the Fall, contends that if they can abolish all divisions and show that everything is equal, then Christianity too must be false, since such divisions lie at the core of the biblical outlook. In their vain fight, these opponents nevertheless always use arguments and standards that assume the truth of Christianity! (Remember the milk buying and hypocrisy mentioned previously.)

Other opponents seek to undo the biblical antithesis by redrawing the divinely imposed line. Instead of dividing between those with Christ and those opposed to Him, they seek to divide humanity by superior and inferior races or classes. They think that those in the allegedly inferior groups cause all social ills and that the way to make things better is to let the "superior races" rule and/or get rid of the "inferiors." But such deep wickedness flies in the face of biblical reality. This ancient ploy is just another attempt to evade God and personal accountability by blaming evil on anyone else apart from those in the "superior" group. In contrast, Christianity recognizes that the distinctions of race and class are irrelevant to questions of sin and salvation. The friends and enemies of God come "out of every tribe and tongue and people and nation" (Rev. 5:9). Like the opponents noted above, these latter opponents of Christianity also invoke all sorts of standards that their outlook cannot justify.

The Fall and Evil

Behind much of the spiritual battle between Christianity and its opponents stand questions of evil. The opponents of Christianity try to account for evil in the world by blaming other races or, among other things, blaming Christianity and Western culture for its divisiveness. Nonetheless, we should find it curious that those who call Christianity evil or profess to reject Christianity because of all the evil in the world, still have to assume the truth of Christianity in order to make those judgments. Whenever we judge that something is good, pleasant, bad, or evil, we always invoke some universal moral standard beyond our personal tastes. Yet non-Christians can't provide an account of the world that can justify using those standards. Certainly evolution and Eastern religions rule out any such standards. So, opponents concerned with evil attack Christianity while having to use Christianity! How futile.

Since we have to assume Christianity to even complain about evil in the world, evil, within a biblical outlook, points us back to the characteristics of God. How do Christians account for evil—the slaughtering earthquakes, mangling accidents, traumatic disloyalties, and so much else? We rest assured in God's lordship over all things. Scripture tells us that sometimes God imposes painful judgment on individuals and cultures because of their rebellion: "If there is calamity in a city, will not the Lord have done it?" (Amos 3:6). Sometimes He does it to strengthen the character of His people. Given the truth of Christianity with a God Who is all-knowing and holy, we know that God has a powerful reason for permitting and bringing about evil in the world. We cannot understand all the reasons behind evil in the world, but we know that God is working "to make known the riches of His glory" (Rom. 9:23).

Most comforting in the face of evil is the Christian confidence that God controls all things, from things that look like chance (Prov. 16:33) to the most pivotal historical events (Acts 2:23). We should be terrified and without hope if something could overcome God's plan. If that were possible, He wouldn't be much more than a big man. But that's not the sort of God Christians worship. The God of the Bible is the God "who works all things according to the counsel of His will" (Eph. 1:11), all the while mysteriously preserving genuine human choice and responsibility (Jn. 12:48). In the midst of evil, God's people have the wonderful assurance that "all things work together for good for those who love God" (Rom. 8:28). Only a sovereign, all-controlling God could accomplish that. Evil could never overwhelm God's purposes.

Creation and the Fall tell us so much about the God of the Bible and the Christian message as a whole. But the most wonderful conclusion yet remains. God had every right to abandon us in our sin after our rebellion. He would be perfectly just to destroy us at any point in our lives. After all, we are the rebels, seeking futilely to dethrone the just God. But God didn't abandon us in our self-deceived misery. He provided an astonishing way out—redemption.

paradise regained:
Christ's redemptive work

Given, lost, and regained—that's the pattern of the Christian message. Through Adam, humans were in fellowship with God, then Adam, our representative, sold his descendants into slavery and destitution, and now Christ, our representative, has purchased His descendants back from slavery to sin. This "purchasing back" of Adam's descendants is one way of summarizing the notion of redemption or paradise regained. To redeem something involves recovering ownership, rescuing, ransoming, and buying back that which was lost. When Christians speak of redemption, they speak of the entire process starting immediately after the Fall to the completed restoration of God and His people in the future, all centering around Christ's work on the cross.

Redemption Anticipated

Every good book has a backbone that ties everything together. The Bible is no different. From the beginning to the end of Scripture, one repeated promise stands out as that connecting backbone, namely, God's promise that "I will be your God, and you shall be My people." So much depth lies in that short promise that we can spend lifetimes appreciating its beauty and glory. It brings to mind the union and harmony humans once had with God, the bond of care and closeness between a good father and His children. It highlights the power of the sovereign God who can command and assuredly bring about such a bond in the face of all historical obstacles. And it reminds us of God's division between His friends inside that bond and His enemies outside it.

This primary promise connects all the major episodes during the anticipation of redemption in the early part of Scripture, prior to the arrival of Christ. This promise builds subtly, then more explicitly, and then most gloriously throughout the prophets of the Old Covenant. For a better grasp of Christianity, we can follow this primary promise of redemption through the most prominent Old Testament figures: Adam, Noah, Abraham, Moses, David, and the major prophets.

Adam: Immediately after the Fall, God justly pronounced a curse upon Adam and Eve and their descendants. In the midst of the anguish of this curse (Gen. 3:14–19) and after the divine imposition of enmity, hostility, between God's people and His enemies, God mercifully anticipated His redemption of His people by promising that someone from the woman "shall bruise"—crush and overwhelm—the serpent's head and that the serpent will bruise that descendant's heel. From the very beginning, then, we are told to expect a redeemer who will crush the enemy of God but in so doing that redeemer too will be harmed.

Noah: From Adam and Noah, the battle raged between the seed of the woman and the seed of the serpent. Finally God poured out His judgment on all creation by means of a flood that reduced the world population back down to one family once again, a family who had descended from the faithful seed of the woman (Gen. 5). As with Adam, God commanded Noah to be fruitful and multiply. Also as with Adam, God made a covenant with Noah as the representative of all his descendants and all the living creatures (Gen. 9:9). God promised never to destroy all life by a flood again and commanded Noah to impose the death penalty on anyone who murdered another human. With creation and society thus preserved by this covenant, God could then develop the promise of the coming redemption.

Abraham: From the faithful descendants of Noah (the seed of the woman) descended Abraham (or Abram as he was first called). God commanded Abraham to be faithful, and Abraham obeyed, leaving his country for another (Gen. 12). God made a covenant with Abraham and gave that primary promise of being the God of Abraham and his descendants and they His people—"I will establish My covenant between Me and you and your descendants after you . . . and I will be their God" (Gen. 17:7–8). Here also we learn that this primary promise is explained in terms of promises to Abraham of a *land* and a *people*. Most significantly in terms of these promises, God promised that in Abraham "all the families of the earth shall be blessed" (Gen. 12:3; cf. 15:5; 17:5–6). Centuries later, the New Testament identified this promise of worldwide blessings through Abraham as the *Christian gospel* (Gal. 3:8)—here is the

Jewishness of Christianity indeed! But Abraham never saw the fulfillment of these promises. Instead God called Abraham to trust Him, and, to confirm these promises to Abraham, God made an oath, an elaborate blood oath testifying that God would accomplish His promises on pain of death, God's own death (Gen. 15)! Astounding as it may seem, such a divine death was ultimately required so many centuries later in order to fulfill the eternal promises to Abraham.

Moses: God also promised Abraham that his later descendants would suffer in slavery for a time, though the promise of a land and a people would stand firm. Later while the descendants of Abraham suffered under Egyptian slavery, God called out Moses and declared through him to the Israelites that "I will bring you out from under the burdens of the Egyptians . . . *I will take you as My people, and I will be your God.* . . . I will bring you into the land which I swore to give to Abraham" (Exod. 6:6–8). Notice that that primary promise shows up in this passage.

So God renewed His covenant with the descendants of Abraham, and as with Abraham (Gen. 18:19), God required that His people obey His precious commandments, trusting in Him with all their being (Deut. 6:4) and loving each other as each loves himself (Lev. 19:18, 34). To help His people even more, God gave them civil and church leaders and a written inscription of His commands for wisdom in every area of life. At such wisdom, even non-Israelite nations would marvel— "What great nation is there that has such statutes and righteous judgments as are in all this law which I set before you this day?" (Deut. 4:8). No other nation's wisdom could even compare to the gracious insights in God's commands. What a gift! Still, though, God warned them that they, Israel, ought not to become arrogant, but remain humble, loving, faithful, and thankful to their gracious God.

Included in these commandments was an elaborate system of animal sacrifices that would serve as a continuous reminder to Israel that *sin always deserves death.* God was so holy that He could not bear to be in the presence of sin, and so the people could only approach their God by symbolically having their sins transferred to another, an animal substitute who would take their just punishment—a substitutionary atonement. This form of substitutionary atonement made up the heart of Old Covenant thinking. A just God cannot be at peace with man so long as man is marred by sin. Sin has to be judged and separated from the people of God in order for true harmony and peace to triumph. The centrality of blood atonement in the Old Covenant also shows us why the religion of Islam is not a serious option, since Islam claims to follow in the Abrahamic tradition, but it openly repudiates any need for blood atonement, thus cutting itself off from the heart of biblical faith.

As with every covenant, God set down conditions for Israel as well. If the people of Israel trusted God and showed their faith by their obedience to His commands, then God promised to be close to them and bless them in every area of life as a father to a child (Deut. 28:1–14). But if they rebelled and refused His graciousness, then He would pour out His covenantal curses on them (Deut. 28:15–68). Nonetheless, successive generations of Abraham's descendants broke God's covenant and rebelled against its every provision. They preferred darkness to light and repeatedly invited God's wrath on themselves. They would not and could not remain faithful, except for a remnant. Their sacrifices were merely external, and they needed inner renewal and power to remain faithful. For a complete fulfillment of the gospel, God declared to Abraham they would have to wait, and wait they did especially for a unique prophet. As Moses foretold, "the Lord your God will raise up for you a Prophet like me from your midst, from your brethren. Him you shall hear" (Deut. 18:15). At every step in the anticipation of redemption, we learn more about God's goodness and justice, and we continue to learn more about this promised one who will conquer the serpent, bring worldwide blessings of a land and a people, and be a faithful and unique prophet of God.

David: After the passing of Moses, Israel continued to battle the seed of the serpent in the form of the surrounding idolatrous nations, and it continued to battle its own internal unfaithfulness. But God did not forget His ancient covenantal promises to Abraham and Moses. Throughout that time, He preserved a faithful remnant, and finally revealed more about Himself by calling forth David, a man after God's own heart. David became the most powerful and famous King of Israel. He glorified God in His triumphs (2 Sam. 7:18) and in His repentance for his own horrid sins (Ps. 51). Through David's many battles with the seed of the serpent, God finally gave him and the people a period of rest from their enemies. David declared that God "remembers His covenant forever . . . the covenant which He made with Abraham, . . . to Israel as an everlasting covenant"

(Ps. 105:8–10). Like his predecessors, David recalled that primary covenantal promise, confessing to God that "You have made Your people Israel Your very own people forever; and You, LORD, have become their God" (2 Sam. 7:24).

God made a special promise to David, seen in only hints before this time. He promised David that "I will set up your seed after you, . . . and I will establish his kingdom. He shall build a house for My name, and I will establish the throne of his kingdom forever. I will be his Father, and he shall be My son. If he commits iniquity, I will chasten him . . . But My mercy shall not depart from him . . . Your throne shall be established forever" (2 Sam. 7:12–16).

God had promised Abraham kings as descendants (Gen. 17:6), but to David, He described a kingly throne extending *forever.* Now it looked as if the ancient Abrahamic promise of a people and a land would be truly fulfilled. But such was not the case. Something more perplexing was afoot. Soon after David's passing, unfaithfulness set in once again. Israel was soon torn asunder with civil war and idolatry. Instead of the promise of worldwide blessing, God nearly destroyed all of Israel, exiling most of the tribes for their rebellion. David's descendants remained in the land for a while, and several faithful kings emerged, but here too idolatry finally prevailed. The people didn't have the ability to remain faithful. So, in the end, God ejected even David's family from the promised land. All of Israel was apparently cut off from the promises to Abraham, Moses, and David. But God said His promises were eternal and that His mercy would always remain with David's line. Something yet was still forthcoming.

The Prophets: In this time of Israel's exile and despair, God raised up many prophets to condemn and encourage the people. And in the prophet's mouths, He recalled His previous promises of a land, a people, and an eternal throne for David, who by then had long passed from the scene.

The prophet Isaiah revealed that God had not completely discarded "the descendants of Abraham" (Is. 41:8; cf. 29:22; 63:16) and that God would indeed "make an everlasting covenant with you [Israel]—the sure mercies of David" (Is. 55:3; cf. 9:7; 16:5). The prophet Jeremiah similarly revealed that God would restore the "descendants of Abraham, Isaac, and Jacob" (Jer. 33:26) so that they would "serve the LORD their God, and David their king, whom I will raise up for them" (Jer. 30:9; cf. 17:25; 21:12). Ezekiel too recalled all the earlier promises when he declared in one passage that God would indeed bring His people to "dwell in the land that I have given to Jacob [Abraham's grandson]" *and* that His people would then keep the commandments given to Moses—"they shall also walk in My judgments and observe My statutes, and do them" *and* that "My servant David shall be their prince forever" (Ezek. 37:24–25).

Moreover, the prophets continued to raise that primary promise spoken so long before. Through Isaiah God reminded Israel, "I am the LORD your God . . . You are My people" (Is. 51:15–16). Through Jeremiah, God testified, "They shall be My people, and I will be their God" (Jer. 32:38). Ezekiel too prophesied, "I, the LORD, will be their God, and My servant David a prince among them; . . . you shall be My people, and I will be your God" (Ezek. 34:24; 36:28).

The prophets also elaborated more on God's good news that through Abraham He would bless *all the families of the earth*. From the beginning, Judaism saw itself as the bearer of God's blessings to *all* the families and nations of the world, not just biological Hebrews alone. The prophets foresaw a day when Gentiles, non-Jews, would come and bow before the God of Abraham. Isaiah saw that "in that day there shall be a root of Jesse [i.e., a descendant of David], who shall stand as a banner to the people; For the Gentiles shall seek Him" (Is. 11:10). Similarly, Isaiah declared that "in the latter days . . . the mountain of the LORD's house shall be established . . . And all nations shall flow to it" (Is. 2:2).

The prophet Amos saw that when the future David would arise, Israel would include "all the Gentiles called by [God's] name" (Amos 9:12). Similarly, the prophet Joel declared God's promise that "it shall come to pass afterward that I will pour out My Spirit on all flesh," all mankind (Joel 2:28). The passages go on and on. The prophets point to the time when the Gentiles would receive redemption from the Lord in fulfillment of His promises to Abraham.

The distinctive feature of this future inclusion of the Gentiles is that God will *empower* His people to be faithful. Unlike Israelites of old who continually turned from their gracious God, the new Israel, made up of Jews *and* Gentiles will be empowered to obey. Most significantly, Jeremiah spoke of this future time as the time of the New Covenant of which God declared

> Behold the days are coming, says the LORD, when
> I will make a new covenant with the house of Is-
> rael and with the house of Judah—not according
> to the covenant that I made with their fathers . . .
> My covenant which they broke, though I was a
> husband to them, says the LORD. But this is the
> covenant that I will make with the house of Israel
> . . . I will put My law in their minds, and write it
> on their hearts; and *I will be their God, and they
> shall be My people.* (Jer. 31:31–33)

This future covenant would not be like the older covenant where the people could not be faithful. In this
New Covenant, God Himself would ensure their faithfulness by planting His commandments on their minds
and writing His law on their hearts. They would have a
new inner ability to obey God, quite different from that
of Israel of old. Ezekiel, too, spoke of the coming new
era when the power of God's Spirit would transform
His people:

> I will sprinkle clean water on you, and you shall
> be clean; I will cleanse you from all your filthi-
> ness and from all your idols. I will give you a new
> heart and put a new spirit within you; I will take
> the heart of stone out of your flesh and give you
> a heart of flesh. I will put My Spirit within you
> and cause you to walk in My statutes, and you
> will keep My judgments and do them. Then you
> shall dwell in the land that I gave to your fathers;
> *you shall be My people, and I will be your God.*
> (Ezek. 36:25–28)

Such passages provide a glorious view of the new era,
when God would pour out His Spirit on His people,

Jew and Gentile alike. But such promises also suggest a dilemma. How could God pour out His Spirit on a corrupt people? How could a *holy* God be in such intimate communion with a *sinful* people? Scripture repeatedly shows us that God cannot just overlook sin, like a weak parent. God's justice and righteousness demand that sin be punished by death. So how can God promise to pour out His Spirit on a people so corrupted by sin? The prophet Isaiah and all the Old Covenant promises and ceremonies point us to the answer—God will provide a perfect substitute to take the punishment for His people. Through Isaiah especially, God foretold of a special servant:

> Behold My servant shall deal prudently; He shall be exalted and extolled and be very high. . . . So shall He sprinkle many nations. Kings shall shut their mouths at Him; . . . Surely He has borne our griefs and carried our sorrows; yet we esteemed Him stricken, smitten by God, and afflicted. But He was wounded for our transgressions, He was bruised for our iniquities; The chastisement for our peace was upon Him, and by His stripes we are healed. All we like sheep have gone astray; we have turned, every one to his own way; and the Lord has laid on Him the iniquity of us all. . . . For the transgressions of My people He was stricken. . . . Yet it pleased the LORD to bruise Him; He has put Him to grief. When you make His soul an offering for sin, He shall see His seed, He shall prolong His days, and the pleasure of the Lord shall prosper in His hand. He shall see the labor of His soul, and be satisfied. By His knowledge My righteous servant shall justify many, for He shall bear their iniquities. (Is. 52:13–53:11)

This is the glorious divine resolution of the problem of God's justice! God would provide a righteous substitute to take the punishment of His people. He would be in close harmony and peace with His people, pouring out His transforming Spirit on them, by punishing the substitute who would represent His people. Adam lost our communion with God, but this representative would redeem it back.

In this one divine servant, we find the anticipated answer to God's promises to Adam, Abraham, Moses, and David—all in one—a future servant who would conquer the seed of the serpent, bring blessings to all nations and families, prophesy like Moses, rule righteously and peacefully in the line of David, and suffer death as the substitute blood sacrifice for His people. By such a divine servant, God could truly then repair Adam's ruin and declare that primary promise to His people, "I will be your God and you shall be My people." But all this was merely promised in anticipation, the reality was still to come.

Redemption Secured

With such a glorious anticipation, the people of God waited the fulfillment of all the ancient promises. When we turn from the pages of the Old Covenant or Testament to the pages of the New Covenant, we find that long after the death of the older Israelite prophets, a messenger from God returned to pronounce the glorious fulfillment of the covenantal promises to a young, faithful woman: "Behold you will conceive in your womb and bring forth a son, and shall call his name

Jesus. He will be great, and will be called the Son of the Highest; and the Lord God will give Him the throne of His father David. And He will reign over the house of Jacob forever, and of His kingdom there will be no end" (Lk. 1:31–33). Mary herself recognized this as God's fulfillment of His ancient promises to Abraham: "He has helped His servant Israel, in remembrance of His mercy, as He spoke to our fathers, to Abraham and to his seed forever" (Lk. 1:54–55).

Christ Himself confessed to being the long-awaited Messiah (Jn. 4:26) and said, "Abraham rejoiced to see My day" (Jn. 8:56). Christ's Apostles, too, explained His covenantal connection to Abraham, Moses, and David. The Apostle Peter preached to the people that "You are the sons of the prophets, and of the covenant which God made with our father, saying to Abraham, 'And in your seed all the families of the earth shall be blessed.' To you first, God having raised up His Servant Jesus, sent Him to bless you, in turning away every one of you from your iniquities" (Acts 3:25–26). In the same way, Peter declared that Christ was *the* Prophet promised by Moses (Acts 3:22) and that David knew that God would "raise up the Christ to sit on his throne" (Acts 2:30).

Significantly as well, the early Christians recognized the coming of Christ as the initiation of the New Covenant and saw this *better* covenant as the fulfillment of that primary promise, "I will be their God, and they shall be My people" (Heb. 8:10; 1 Cor. 6:18).

Sacrificial Substitute: At the very core of securing a restored relationship between God and His people stands the need for bloodshed. Before the redemptive blessings promised to Abraham could go to all the world, the people had to be truly cleared of sin. And this bloodshed couldn't be the sort of symbolic, ineffective animal sacrifices of the Old Covenant. Those were shadows of what God demanded. In the end, only a true human, not a mere animal, could stand in the place of humans. Such a human substitute had to be innocent himself, or else he too would deserve death. So, Christ's central mission was to serve as the blameless, sacrificial Lamb of God to "save His people from their sins" (Mt. 1:21) by being sacrificed on the Cross at Calvary. He Himself said that He had come "to serve and give His life a ransom for many" (Mt. 20:28). Just as Isaiah had prophesied, "for the transgressions of My people He was stricken" (Is. 53:8). In the same way that the sacrifices of the Old Covenant were for a particular people of God's choosing and not for those outside the covenant, so too did Christ die to save His particular people, His church (Acts 20:28), now taken from all nations and tribes.

The Bible describes Christ's sacrifice as a *propitiation,* an important term that speaks of *a sacrifice that turns away the wrath, the anger, of God.* Given the Fall of man, we know that God is angry with humans for their senseless rebellion. Our sin calls out for God's judgment. But God, in His mercy, displayed His love by sending Christ as a propitiation for sin. The Apostle John said, "the love of God was manifested toward us, that God sent His only begotten Son into the world, that we might live through Him. In this is love, not that we loved God, but that He loved us and sent His Son to be the propitiation for our sins" (1 Jn. 4:9–10).

God's people can justly be at peace with God, because His holy wrath has been poured out on their substitute, Jesus Christ crucified on the cross.

As the Apostle Paul explained, Christ's gracious propitiation shows us the justice and the love of God in one pivotal event: "All have sinned and fall short of the glory of God, being justified freely by His grace through the redemption that is Christ Jesus, whom God set forth as a propitiation by His blood, through faith, to demonstrate His righteousness, because in His forbearance God had passed over the sins that were previously committed, to demonstrate at the present time His righteousness, that He might be the just and the justifier of the one who has faith in Jesus" (Rom. 3:23–26). Christ's sacrifice alone effectively turns away God's just wrath. We can find peace and life only by submitting to Christ as our merciful substitute. Those who wholeheartedly trust in Christ and not in any of their own corrupted and impotent "righteousness," are those at peace with God.

Justification: Christ's sacrificial work includes even more. Christ's propitiatory sacrifice is the means by which God forgives our sin, the means by which He *justifies* us, authoritatively declaring us not guilty of our crimes. The Bible is full of the language of justification, and these many descriptions tell us that justification is what takes place in a courtroom. For example, God declared in His law that the purpose of a good judge is to "justify the righteous and condemn the wicked" (Deut. 25:1). Such a judge doesn't make a person clean or inwardly holy; his justification of the accused is an authoritative legal judgment or declaration—"Not guilty!"

The threat of judicial condemnation no longer hangs over that person; he is forgiven. This is part of what God has done through Christ. He has justified—authoritatively removed His condemnation from His people.

But God cannot just overlook our flagrant and deep rebellion and arbitrarily declare us not guilty. That would be contrary to His holy nature. In order to declare us not guilty, He *imputed* or covenantally attributed His people's sin to their New Covenant representative, Jesus Christ; and in turn, God has imputed or attributed our guilt to Christ—a gracious double imputation! Christ is declared legally guilty for our sin, and we are declared not guilty by His perfect righteousness. As the Scripture explains: "For He [God] made Him [Christ] who knew no sin to be sin for us, that we might become the righteousness of God in Him" (2 Cor. 5:21). And on this just basis, God can justify the ungodly, those who have no righteousness of their own.

This path from paradise lost to paradise regained involved a wonderful reversal of Adam's rebellion. Adam represented his descendants, and He was a "type of Him who was to come" (Rom. 5:14). As noted earlier, when Adam rebelled, his descendants became guilty by imputation—"through one man's offense judgment came to all men, resulting in condemnation" (Rom. 5:18). Where Adam was disobedient to His covenant with God, Christ was obedient—"I have kept My Father's commandments and abide in His love" (Jn. 15:10). Where Adam failed, Christ, "the second Adam," succeeded—"For as in Adam all die, even so in Christ all shall be made alive" (1 Cor. 15:22). Like Adam, Christ represented His descendants, but instead of imputing condemnation, Christ imputed righteousness—"as by one man's disobedience many were made sinners, so also by one Man's obedience many will be made righteous" (Rom. 5:19).

All of this would be of no help though if Christ remained in the grave after His sacrifice on the cross. If death conquered our representative, then it would still conquer us as well. If death conquered Christ, then He too was enslaved to the consequences of sin. But the glorious truth of Christ is that He conquered death and its consequences and rose from the dead—death could not hold Him! He had no sin of His own to tie Him in the grave, and so as Adam brought death for His sin, Christ brought back eternal life by His sinlessness. And since Christ is the covenant representative of His people, they will rise again as well. Christ's resurrection revealed His holiness (Acts 2:24–36) and justified His people (Rom. 4:25; 1 Cor. 15:17).

So Christians can confess with the Apostle Paul that we are now in Christ, "not having [our] own righteousness . . . but that which is through faith in Christ, the righteousness which is from God by faith" (Phil. 3:9). The righteousness with which we can stand before God is not our own; it is an alien righteousness, Christ's righteousness, a perfect righteousness so that "there is therefore now no condemnation to those who walk in Christ Jesus" (Rom. 8:1). As David said long ago: "Blessed is he whose transgression is forgiven, whose sin is covered. Blessed is the man to whom the Lord does not impute iniquity" (Ps. 32:1–2). This is the glory of the Christian gospel. Christ's work turns away God's wrath, and God imputes our sin to Christ and Christ's righteousness to us. And since our salvation is anchored in the perfect and complete work of Christ and not in ourselves, we can have great assurance that our redemption is unfailing and secure. What a wonder! What a powerful reversal of the Fall!

But this justification isn't automatically given to everyone. Those outside of Christ are still under God's just condemnation. To receive justification, one must become united to Christ, under His covenantal representation, *by faith*. Faith is the instrument whereby we receive Christ's perfect righteousness and can be at peace with God. Faith is not merely an intellectual acceptance of these truths (Jas. 2:18–19). Faith in Christ is a wholehearted trust and dependence upon Christ's work, not our own, for reconciliation with God. Such faith is just like Abraham's, Moses', and David's, a trusting in God's righteousness. Such faith is like that of a small child to a parent. The child does not earn or merit the parent's love. The parent creates the relationship by giving birth, quite apart from the efforts of the child. The child trusts fully in the parent for life and everything. And the best children show their gratitude not by mere words but by faithfully trying to please and obey the parent. They reveal their faith by their obedience—"faith without works is dead" (Jas. 2:26). But faith is not the ground, the foundation, of our salvation; it is merely the means. The ground of our salvation is Christ's perfect work on the cross.

Still a question should arise. If in the Fall, all became rebellious and dead in their sin, how can they ever hope to have faith? Dead bodies can't respond well at all. How can Adam's spiritually dead descendants work up the effort to trust in Christ for justification? The answer is that they can't, but God can raise the dead.

Redemption Applied

Out on a bleak valley in ancient Babylon during Israel's exile, God took hold of His prophet Ezekiel. God showed Ezekiel a valley full of dead men's bones drying in the sun (Ezek. 37). Then He told Ezekiel to do something very odd—to *preach* to the bones. By means of that preaching, God turned this valley of dead men into a living, vibrant army of His people. In the same way, the Holy Spirit gives life to the dead, sight to the blind, faith to the rebellious. But what is this Holy Spirit? I've previously spoken of the Father and the Son but not the Holy Spirit. Where does this Spirit fit in?

Ezekiel is a good place to start, since He prophesied of the coming of the Holy Spirit in the time of the New Covenant. As noted earlier in this essay, God had promised that in the new era, "I will put My Spirit within you and cause you to walk in My statutes" (Ezek. 36:27). Jeremiah prophesied similarly (Jer. 31:31–35). But the prophet Joel spoke most explicitly about the coming of the Holy Spirit—"it shall come to pass afterward that I will pour out My Spirit on all flesh; your sons and daughters shall prophesy; your old men shall dream dreams; your young men shall see visions" (Joel 2:28). This is a picture of great spiritual blessings in contrast with the Old Covenant. The New Covenant people would be filled with the Spirit of God in a way relatively unknown in the Old. In the Old, God dwelt with His people in a limited way through a temple, cut off from them by walls and curtains and regulations. But in the New Covenant, God would dwell in His people in a special, empowering way. This is the outpouring of the Holy Spirit that the Apostles recognized after Christ returned to heaven.

But the Holy Spirit isn't some impersonal cosmic force. The Holy Spirit is a distinct person, as the Son of God and the Father are distinct persons. In biblical thinking we are confronted with an awesome mystery about God. Christianity is monotheistic; we believe in one God (1 Cor. 4:8). The Scripture reveals that this one God is also three distinct persons, Father, Son, and Holy Spirit (Mt. 28:19). God is three-in-one, a tri-unity, or a Trinity. These supreme persons are not three Gods or three aspects of one God. The three are all equally God in power, but have taken on different tasks in history. The Son, though equal to the Father (Phil. 2:5), submitted Himself and took on a human body (Jn. 1:1, 14) in order to represent humans as Adam did. The Holy Spirit, in turn, came after the work of the Son (Jn. 16:7) in order to empower and apply the redemption secured by Christ.

So when we speak of redemption applied, we speak of the work of the third person of the Trinity, the Holy Spirit. As above, the Spirit begins to apply redemption by enabling spiritually dead sinners to turn to Christ in faith (Tit. 3:5; Eph. 2:1, 5; Col. 2:13; Acts 16:14). Following this, the Spirit then works to transform us on the inside. Justification removes God's condemnation from us, but does nothing to us internally. Justification removes our guilt but not our sinfulness. After justification, God's people need to be renewed and transformed inwardly. This process of growing in godliness is known as *sanctification*, and it is the battle Christians fight to their dying day.

Sanctification: As everyone can testify, Christians don't become godly overnight, though they may now want to. Christians, though justified, will continue to fight against sin in their lives just as a legally victorious army may have to fight pockets of resistance long after the war has ended. Christians have been freed from the enslaving domination of sin that they experienced as non-Christians. Now they serve a new master, Christ.

The goal of sanctification is for every Christian to imitate the godliness found in Christ, our primary model. He glorified God in everything and obeyed God's commands sincerely, from the heart. His was a life dominated by loving God and loving His neighbor.

More specifically, the Holy Spirit aims to produce virtues in God's people, virtues that ought to distinguish them from all other communities. Scripture describes these virtues as "the fruit of the Spirit"—namely "love, joy, peace, longsuffering, kindness, goodness, faithfulness, gentleness, self-control" (Gal. 5:22–23). Nothing is more important for Christian living than to honor God by pursuing the fruit of the Spirit. Everything else is worthless if the Christian isn't daily attempting to exhibit the fruit of the Spirit. Our constant prayer should be for the Spirit's help in bringing these to a living reality. The entire goal of God's plan of creation, Fall, redemption is designed to produce a godly and faithful people for the glory of God. Christ taught that we should "seek first the kingdom of God and His righteousness" (Mt. 6:31).

In another context Paul explained that a Christian life *not* dominated by genuine, biblical love is not truly Christian:

> And though I have the gift of prophecy, and understand all mysteries and all knowledge, and though I have all faith, so that I could move mountains, *but have not love, I am nothing.* And though I bestow all my goods to feed the poor and though I give my body to be burned, but have not love, it profits me nothing. (1 Cor. 13:2–3)

Over and over again, Scripture exhorts God's people to true Christian living, to true fruitfulness in the Spirit. Any Christian who doesn't have this as his chief priority under God is malformed in some way. The Christian that shows neither fruit of the Spirit nor concern for it reveals that perhaps the Spirit was never planted so as to give rise to the fruit. "Christians" that have their priorities so out of order that they fight bitterly show their lack of the Spirit. Christians can and do disagree over many things, but true Christians can disagree respectfully and in accord with the fruit of the Spirit. The tragedy of gross hypocrisy among contemporary Christianity highlights Christ's own promise that "not everyone who says to Me, 'Lord, Lord,' shall enter the kingdom of heaven, but he who does the will of My father in heaven" (Mt. 7:21).

Godliness Exercised: The Holy Spirit aids us in our sanctification—our growth in godliness—through various means. The Apostle Paul exhorts, "exercise yourself toward godliness" (1 Tim. 4:7). As athletes exercise their bodies through physical discipline, Christians are to exercise themselves through spiritual discipline. Throughout Scripture, the faithful discipline themselves by such regular means as prayer, Scripture reading and meditation, fasting, care for others, worship, and much more. The Holy Spirit uses all these things to discipline us into godliness. We train so as to replace our non-Christian habits with Christian habits, so that our tempers and reactions will be more and more like Christ's. But such a lifelong effort takes lifelong discipline, and anyone that seeks to live the Christian life without discipline is begging for disaster.

Nurturing the fruit of the Spirit, and especially love, does not mean that Christians are emotional jellyfish or sheepish—always being weak and never strong-minded. At times, genuine Christian love necessitates rebuke and anger. Christ showed anger and so did the Apostle Paul. Each response has its place. We are exhorted that "as much depends upon you, live peaceably with all men" (Rom. 12:18). Some things deserve anger and some don't. One means that God has given for discerning priorities is His law, the standard of sanctification.

The Standard of Sanctification: The Apostle James tells us that the person "who looks into the perfect law of liberty and continues in it, and is not a forgetful hearer but a doer of the work, this one will be blessed in what he does" (Jas. 1:25). God's law given to Moses is that "perfect law of liberty." It forms the standards for Christian behavior and shows us our priorities. We may have been conditioned not to think of commandments as liberating in the way James does, but this is a modern failing. God's commandments are somewhat like railroad tracks to a train. Without tracks the train goes nowhere easily, but with sleek rails, the train has great liberty. Humans often try to encumber God's liberating commands with their own man-made additions and traditions, and these received some of Christ's sharpest rebukes.

The Apostle Paul described God's law as "holy and just and good." (Rom. 7:12). Christ declared that "Whoever therefore breaks one of the least of these commandments, and teaches men so, shall be called least in the kingdom of heaven; but whoever does and teaches them, he shall be called great in the kingdom of heaven" (Mt. 5:19). Much earlier, David glorified God for the profound wisdom revealed in these laws: "Oh, how I love Your law! It is my meditation all the day. You, through Your commandments make me wiser than my enemies . . . I will walk at liberty, for I seek your precepts" (Ps. 119:97–98, 45).

The fruit of the Spirit and God's law go hand in hand. Christ's Apostles defined love as keeping the law. Love is not some shapeless, subjective emotion. Love means that we treat others in accord with God's commands: we don't murder, envy, or steal from them. As the Apostle Paul says, "Love does no harm to a neighbor; therefore love is the fulfillment of the law" (Rom. 13:10). Similarly the Apostle John says, "by this we know that we love the children of God, when we love God and keep His commandments. For this is the love of God, that we keep His commandments. And His commandments are not burdensome" (1 Jn. 5:2–3).

Sanctified Worldview: The sanctification discussed above cannot be limited just to the inner, meditative life of an individual. God is the Lord over all things not just our inner life. He is Lord over our families, work, recreation, education, economics, civil affairs, art, philosophy, science, and every other feature of life. Since God is Lord over these things, we are to take part to God's glory—"whether you eat or drink, or whatever you do, do all to the glory of God" (1 Cor. 10:31). In truth every philosophy or outlook does this sort of thing. Every outlook has some ultimate principle in terms of which it understands the world. Humanists look at all of life in humanistic terms. Hindus and New Agers do so in accord with their principles. So we should expect that Christians will also have a "Christian view" of history, art, politics, philosophy, and so forth.

So when we wish to figure out a Christian understanding of abortion, euthanasia, property questions, taxation, foreign policy, we naturally look to the Scriptures. After all, we're told that "all Scripture . . . is profitable for doctrine, reproof, for correction, for instruction in righteousness that the man of God may be thoroughly equipped for every good work" (1 Tim. 3:16). Scripture, therefore, equips us to understand and make judgments about every issue under God. Of course, much work still needs to be done in many areas, but much work has already been done.

The Church: Central to all of Christian sanctification stands the Church. Christ didn't establish a disjointed, individualistic people; He established a covenantal community—the Church—a community of those in submission to Christ and each other, a community that shares the bonds of faith and family and service and worship. As a community under Christ, the Church ought to seek to glorify God first of all, not their own selfish whims.

It ought to worship God in the way God prescribed and not according to vain imaginations.

Within this community of believers, Christ established authoritative officers, elders, who preside over the regular teaching and exposition of Scripture. They oversee the worship of God in the Church and seek to remove scandalous hypocrites from the privileges of the community. The elders are called to guard the gospel and the people from abuse and false teachings. They are called to be like Christ Himself, forever concerned to serve and encourage the people of God. Alongside elders, the Church has other officers, deacons, given over to day-to-day needs of the community, from poverty relief to caring for the sick.

In all, the Church is supposed to be a sanctifying community in which we grow by God-honoring worship, the proclamation of God's word, Church ceremonies (like baptism and the Lord's supper), and close fellowship with other believers of like mind.

Of course, the Christian Church has faced numerous challenges over the centuries. It has faced gross unfaithfulness within its ranks and challenges from unbelief outside. Nonetheless, we are confident that the Church will prosper wonderfully, growing beyond all the divisions we see today, for as Christ promised "the gates of Hades shall not prevail against it" (Mt. 16:18); that is, the Church will win out over all its enemies. For the fulfillment of that promise, we look to the future of redemption, the subject of our final section.

Redemption Fulfilled

In the pattern of creation, Fall, redemption, we've seen God's glorious work in the distant past and present. How will the future of redemption turn out? It gets even better.

Though many contemporary popular expressions of Christianity expect the end of history to arrive with massive disasters, wars, and a nearly extinguished Church, this was not always the case, and a sober understanding of Scripture doesn't lead one in those paths. Historic Protestants have long looked to God's promises rather than the newspapers to get a glimpse of the future.

Standing at the forefront for our understanding of the future is God's still incompletely fulfilled promise to Abraham—"in you all the families of the earth shall be blessed" (Gen. 12:3). Abraham's faithful seed has expanded far beyond the blood relatives of Abraham into the Christian Church spread throughout the world, but Christianity is far from being a blessing in *all* of the earth as was repeatedly promised.

When we look to the Old Covenant prophets, their understanding of the future includes more than just the inclusion of the Gentiles into the people of God. Their vision is that of a worldwide success of biblical faith *before* the end of history.

Most famously, the prophet Isaiah spoke in poetic terms of a future in which peace and faithfulness prevail: "The wolf also shall dwell with the lamb; the leopard shall lie down with the young goat . . . They shall not hurt nor destroy in all My holy mountain, for the earth shall be full of the knowledge of the LORD as the waters cover the sea" (Is. 11:6,9; cf. 2:2–4). Through

Isaiah, God also promised Israel, "I will give you as a light to the Gentiles, that you should be My salvation to the ends of the earth" (Is. 49:6; cf. 54:4–5; 66:12). David declared of the Messiah, "All the ends of the world shall remember and turn to the Lord, and all the families of the nations shall worship before You. For the kingdom is the Lord's, and He rules over the nations" (Ps. 22:27–28; cf. 72:8–20; 102:15).

Malachi prophesied that "from the rising of the sun, even to its going down, My name shall be great among the Gentiles; In every place incense shall be offered to My name, and a pure offering; For My name shall be great among the nations" (Mal. 1:11).

Jeremiah spoke of such a wide expansion of faith that we would not need to teach one another: "Behold the days are coming, says the Lord, when I will make a new covenant. . . . No more shall every man teach his neighbor saying, 'Know the LORD,' for they all shall know Me, from the least of them to the greatest" (Jer. 31:31, 34).

This vision provides a better understanding of the fulfillment of the Abrahamic promises of a land and a people. The land actually promised to Abraham was not merely a small tract on the Mediterranean but the whole world, or as the Apostle Paul says, Abraham was "heir of the world" (Rom. 4:13). And the people promised to Abraham would be so numerous that we can truly speak of Abraham blessing all the families of the earth. In a Christian view of the future of redemption, we should expect a worldwide success for Christianity—not by impotent physical weapons or ballot-box coercion, but by peacefully proclaiming the gospel at home and throughout the world. This may take thousands of years, but history is on our side, because the sovereign God is still fulfilling His ancient covenantal promises. He cannot fail. In this light, then, we can better understand Christ's teaching, "For God so loved the world that He gave His only begotten Son . . . God did not send His Son into the world to condemn the world, but that the world through Him might be saved" (Jn. 3:16–17).

At the end of the Bible, in Revelation 21, we see paradise truly regained in a vision intentionally reminiscent of the Garden of Eden (vv. 10–21). It is a vision of Christ's Church, united, whole, and complete, adorned for Her husband, Christ. It is a vision of the Church as the "holy Jerusalem" (21:2, 10) and with gates named for the twelve tribes of Israel (21:12) on a foundation of the Apostles (21:14). As Ezekiel foretold, God's blessings will so prevail some day that people will say, "This land that was desolate has become like the Garden of Eden" (Ezek. 36:35)—*paradise regained!* Most significantly in this vision of the Church, Christ repeats that primary promise: "Behold the tabernacle of God is with men, and He will dwell with them, and they shall be His people. God Himself will be with them and be their God" (Rev. 21:3–4).

Though Christians may disagree over this or any vision of the end, all Christians agree that Christ will one day return to earth in judgment, resurrecting everyone who has died previously, His friends and enemies alike. He will once and for all separate the faithful seed of the woman from the ever-rebellious seed of the serpent. Christ will finally and justly exile His enemies by sending them into their final horror, hell, complete separation from God's goodness.

His faithful friends, those who trusted in His righteousness and not their own, He will welcome into everlasting union and communion with Father, Son, and Holy Spirit, a relationship than Adam had and beyond our most creative imagination.

Creation, Fall, redemption—that is the pattern of history, all wrapped around God's promise: "I will be their God, and they shall be My people." God gave Adam paradise for us all; then Adam and we rebelled; then Christ faithfully restored it all and then some.

I hope this brief scraping of the surface of Christianity has been helpful in some way. Please remember that just by getting through a booklet like this shows that you are assuming the truth of Christianity. Reading, like the milk buying mentioned at the beginning, assumes the truth of the Christian framework. Trust in Christ and flee from your self-deception—God can be Your God, and you one of His people. As David said so many centuries ago:

> Serve the LORD with fear, and rejoice with trembling. Kiss the Son, lest He be angry, and you perish in the way, when His wrath is kindled but a little. Blessed are all those who put their trust in Him. (Ps. 2:11–12)

more from canon press

For some, it is offensive to think that the Christian faith
has at its very center a mystery, an incomprehensible
truth. To them, Christians seem to be calling for a sacrifice of the intellect on the altar of religious confession.
In reality, trinitarian faith demands something quite
different. It is not a sacrifice of the intellect, but the
sacrifice of *the pretense of intellectual autonomy:* the
notion that the mind or reason of man is the ultimate
judge of truth. The truth of the Trinity requires us to
accept what we cannot fully comprehend. Why should
that be thought so extraordinary? There is no branch of
knowledge, be it physics or biology or history or litera-
ture, that does not confront us with paradox in some
form or other. Why should the Christian doctrine of
God the triune Creator be any less difficult to state and
comprehend than truths of physical science or postula-
tions of secular philosophy?

Trinity & Reality
An Introduction to the Christian Faith
Ralph A. Smith